Bridal Flowers
BOUQUETS, BOUTONNIERES, CORSAGES

GINNY PARFITT
BILL MURPHY, AIFD
TINA SKINNER

Schiffer Publishing Ltd

4880 Lower Valley Road, Atglen, Pennsylvania 19310

www.fleursfrance.com

Acknowledgements

Special thanks to Sterling Arjona, hand model and photographer's assistant. All photos not otherwise credited were taken by Tina Skinner. Photographers who shared their enthusiasm and eye to make this book possible are listed in the resources section with contact information. They would love to be contacted to record your special event.

Finally, thanks to all the beautiful brides, handsome grooms, and members of happy wedding parties anonymously represented herein. Long after the blush is off the rose, our wishes are with you for a lifetime of wonderful shared happiness.

Other Schiffer Books By The Author:

The Bridal Bouquet Book
0-7643-2197-8, $39.95

Other Schiffer Books on Related Subjects:

Accesorizing the Bride: Vintage Wedding Finery Through the Decades
0-7643-2185-4, $49.95

Vintage Wedding Cake Toppers
0-7643-2172-2, $29.95

Cover images courtesy of Artist i Photography

Copyright © 2010 by Schiffer Publishing, Ltd.
Library of Congress Control Number: 2010924175

Designed by Stephanie Daugherty
Type set in Edwardian Script ITC/Nadall/Aldine721 BT/Gill Sans MT
ISBN: 978-0-7643-3485-6
Printed in China

Schiffer Books are available at special discounts for bulk purchases for sales promotions or premiums. Special editions, including personalized covers, corporate imprints, and excerpts can be created in large quantities for special needs. For more information contact the publisher:

Schiffer Publishing Ltd.
4880 Lower Valley Road
Atglen, PA 19310
Phone: (610) 593-1777; Fax: (610) 593-2002
E-mail: Info@schifferbooks.com

For the largest selection of fine reference books on this and related subjects, please visit our web site at

www.schifferbooks.com

We are always looking for people to write books on new and related subjects. If you have an idea for a book please contact us at the above address.

This book may be purchased from the publisher. Include $5.00 for shipping. Please try your bookstore first. You may write for a free catalog.

In Europe, Schiffer books are distributed by
Bushwood Books
6 Marksbury Ave.
Kew Gardens
Surrey TW9 4JF England
Phone: 44 (0) 20 8392 8585; Fax: 44 (0) 20 8392 9876
E-mail: info@bushwoodbooks.co.uk
Website: www.bushwoodbooks.co.uk

Contents

Introduction

SELECTING YOUR WEDDING FLOWERS

-DONNA THEIMER, AIFD, ICPF

*I*s there a time in a woman's life when she is more beautiful than on her wedding day? Starting at a very early age, most of us ladies have thought about our walk down the aisle. Details from the gown style and color right down to the perfect shade of eye shadow are contemplated for years. And when that special guy pops the question, plans begin to create the most spectacular wedding day ever. It's the task of the professional floral designer to turn those dreams into bouquets that are a reflection of the bride's years of planning.

Today's brides are complex and savvy. They approach the organization of their special day with tips from the Internet, guides from bridal shows, and planning books that provide organizational timelines for orchestrating a beautiful wedding event. Collecting photos of preferred bouquet styles and flower types makes the floral designer's job very easy. Brides are looking for suggestions on flowers that will coordinate with their attendant gowns. They may have a set budget and are looking for alternative floral choices or dual-purpose designs to help keep their floral budget in check. A good floral designer will know how to bring all of your ideas together. Listening to these knowledgeable professionals will guarantee that your wedding flowers will be a reflection of your dreams and desires.

Although bridal gowns are created in a variety of colors, brides are still wearing traditional gowns in all shades of white and ivory. Some brides still opt to carry traditional bouquets created out of all-white and ivory flowers. These traditional brides have a very wide variety of blossom selections at their disposal. White lilies, hydrangea, tulips, roses, and stephanotis all make beautiful presentations. However, the current trend is for the bride to have colorful bouquets. In fact, many brides will not use any white flowers in their bouquets. One creative idea is to have the attendants each carry one type of flower and the bride carry a bouquet that is a compilation of all those flowers. Colorful creations really make a bold statement against the backdrop of an all white or ivory gown.

Attendant dresses come in such a huge range of colors. There is as much variety of possible gown colors as there are flowers! Chocolate brown, smoke grey, aqua blue, watermelon pink, saffron yellow, persimmon orange, cherry red, celery green, and plum just to name a few. How do you decide what floral color combinations go with each respective gown color? As it turns out, it's not that difficult.

Jane DaPrix Photography

Use These Simple Rules
When Selecting Your Bouquet Flowers.

One If the attendants are wearing red, using matching flowers may cause the flowers to blend into the dress in the wedding photos. Select flowers that complement and accent the ladies' dresses. That same red dress would look fantastic with a bouquet created with a variety of flowers in an analogous color combination of red, orange, and yellow. The contrasting floral colors would really be striking against the dresses.

Two Keep your floral color selection in the same color intensity across your palette. If you start with soft, pastel roses, select other pastel flowers to go into the creations. If you like a more intense color combination, use jewel-toned flowers. The important thing to remember is to keep the same color intensity regardless of the floral items you have selected. It makes the designs appear more unified and polished. Floral growers and breeders have developed so many naturally hued materials that it will be easy to coordinate with your special wedding color selections.

Three Cut flowers and foliage come from many locations around the world. Even so, many are considered seasonal. Looking for tulips in October might bring sticker shock. If a specific flower is not available as a fresh product, use fabric botanicals to add to the bouquet. Fantastic fabric flowers are available that are almost impossible to distinguish from real flora. In addition, many high-quality fabric flowers have petals, leaves, and stems that are individually wired, allowing the floral designer to manipulate the blossoms to mimic the real flower.

Four Think seasonally. There are incredible blossom choices available throughout the year, but consider sticking with the flowers that are in season. Spring brides have a huge assortment of bulb flowers, including blue muscari (grape hyacinth), pink and lilac hyacinth, yellow daffodils, and tulips in many colors and varieties. Lilies, stock, and peonies provide loads of color and fragrance options for the summer bride. Fall brides can select from seasonal grasses and pods, berries, and chrysanthemums in every blossom size and color. Crabapples, mini pumpkins, and other small fruits can also be incorporated. Winter weddings bring a variety of holiday greenery and wintry fare. White pine has the holiday fragrance we all adore and holly leaves, and winterberries mixed with roses and stephanotis can be a striking combination for the winter bride.

Five Roses are amazing, versatile, and desirable flowers. A perennial favorite for bridal bouquets, gorgeous roses are available in a wide assortment of solid and dichromatic options. Some roses, such as David Austin roses, have a wonderful floral fragrance. Roses are long lasting, stand up to a variety of weather conditions, and come in a large variety of sizes. Smaller spray roses are a great way to add depth to the bouquet.

Six The old saying, "Something old, something new, something borrowed, something blue," can provide the bride with an opportunity to personalize her bouquet. Most ladies will not wear their mother's bridal gown, however, many are incorporating pieces of mom's gown into their bouquet. Small trinkets such as a special family rosary or charms filled with photos of loved ones who have passed away can be added to make the bouquet a one-of-a-kind design.

INTRODUCTION

Seven   Select a bouquet that is the right size and style for your body type. Multiple bouquet styles are available and they are starting to change. Although brides and their attendants will always use round bouquets, cascade bouquets are making a comeback. This style of bouquet is perfect for the bride who wants a more dramatic bouquet. Cascade bouquets can also help "heighten" and even slenderize the bride. Petite brides should keep their flowers small. Otherwise, the bouquet can be overpowering. Allowing the floral designer to create something different can provide a bride, and her floral creation, with a custom look.

Eight   Think beyond flowers. Along with floral and foliage selections, a floral designer has access to non-floral embellishments that can be added to bouquets. Decorative wires can be strung with crystals or pearls to match the decorations on the bridal gown. Crystal sprays, reflective beads, and multi-faceted rhinestones provide bling. Small feathers, dried pods, and preserved foliages can really add a special touch. These items can be repeated in the boutonnieres, corsages, and wristlets to create a unified look for the entire wedding party.

If budget concerns are creating stress, why not consider designs that can serve double duty. Cylinder vases can be weighted down with decorative marbles to hold the ladies' bouquets at the head table. All of the attendants' bouquets can be placed in the vases to decorate the head table. The unity candle design can be placed in front of the bride and groom at the reception. The altar designs can be transported to the reception to decorate the entranceway or be used on the place card table. Additionally, many churches will decorate the altar with seasonal blooming plants. Using their floral decorations can help you save money on ceremony flowers.

A wedding without flowers would be like a wedding cake without frosting. Creatively designed floral pieces can make your special day truly beautiful. The majority of your wedding photos will include you and your attendants and although flowers are perishable, your floral bouquet selections will live forever in your wedding photos.

www.kimlemaire.com

WHY FLOWERS?

Why Flowers?

In Roman times the bride and groom wore flowered garlands around their necks to symbolize fertility. It's all about fertility, after all. A driving factor behind the parents' decision to spend lots of money and invite people to celebrate riotously when their children marry is to usher in the possibility of grandchildren.

Flowers in hand were once considered an everyday item. In years past, people imagined that plagues were born upon foul breezes, and therefore carried aromatic bunches of flowers and herbs to ward off disease. Nosegays or posies were also standard prior to the 20th century, when bathing and public standards of cleanliness were not common and body odors and the smell of waste might otherwise overwhelm if not for a handy bunch of flowers to maintain one's equilibrium.

Herbs and their edible flowers were also believed to contain other powers. Some, like garlic, were even credited with the ability to ward off evil spirits, so people festooned themselves with the freshest bunches they could obtain.

A favorite wedding bouquet herb from the past is dill, which was said to increase desire. This pretty, fernlike herb was part of every Victorian bridal bouquet. It's said that Queen Victoria, Prince Albert, and their guests all had a nibble of the lust-inducing herb from the queen's nuptial bouquet.

SPRING

FALL

SUMMER

WINTER

SPRING: www.fleursfrance.com, SUMMER: www.fleursfrance.com FALL: Two tones of gerbera daisies are bound by a matching shimmer of ribbon. www.sideeffectsflowers.com and WINTER: Donna Theimer, AIFD, ICPF

Take a Cue from the Season

*I*t's quite likely that the theme of your entire wedding is centered around the time of year you plan to tie the knot. At the very least, your color theme may be driven by the season.

Nature has provided a palette that popular tastes tend to follow. Springtime is associated with the greens we've been longing for, as well as the pastel hues of spring flowers. Featured prominently are the sunny yellows of daffodils and pretty blues, lavenders, and pinks that break forth from spring bulbs. Think daffodils, lilies, and delicate apple and cherry blossoms.

Summer moves the color range into richer tones of reds and oranges, deep blues and purple. Think roses, peonies, zinnias, daisies, and dahlias.

Fall is rich with harvest tones of pumpkin orange and roasted reds, set against a rich background of aged greens and chestnut tones. Mums in every rich, imaginable shade are at your beck and call, along with sunflowers, hypericum berries, roses, and black-eyed Susan.

Finally, wintertime evokes the stark white of pure snow, the promise of evergreens, and the cheery reds of winter berries. Poinsettia and holly add holiday cheer, while amaryllis, roses, camellias, and white stephanotis are the winter workhorses of floral arrangements.

Flowers enter the ceremony and reception as eye-drawing accents, adorning wedding cakes, table centerpieces, and the marriage altar, not to mention the bride. The flowers' importance to the event can't be overrated. Plan a bouquet that works within the season's color theme, though drawn from the fringes to create an accent, something a little more colorful, one shade brighter, or that much richer to stand out.

SIZE MATTERS

Size Matters

Face it, we are a well-fed lot. Most brides are trying to loose that last ten pounds in the months leading up the wedding. Like choosing a purse, a bouquet can accentuate or draw attention away from your waistline. If the waistline is larger than you would like, a bigger bunch of flowers is going to downplay that fact.

Another consideration is the dress. The dress probably cost you more than the flowers, and you do not want to let the bouquet steal the show. These two points are integral. Study images of dress and bouquet combinations to find the one that works with you. You might even try some mock-ups with your florist beforehand. Bring the dress or a picture of you in it.

www.fleursfrance.com

How to Hold a Bouquet

How to Hold a Bouquet

Do not swing it like a club, or clench it in two hands like a baseball bat. This pretty bouquet, professionally assembled and bound for your event, is not delicate. You are!

While the cascading bouquets of yesterday that all but covered a bride's dress are slowly finding favor again, smaller, hand-tied bouquets are more popular today. These arrangements are far more compact and allow a lot more bride to show.

You have been primped and prepared for this big day. Your body has been waxed, your makeup perfectly applied, and your hands manicured to look their very prettiest. You're not a foil to your bouquet. It's a prop to accentuate your loveliness.

Use the bouquet to show off the work that has been done to prepare you for your moment in the spotlight. Properly held in two hands, the wide stem of your bouquet is an opportunity to show your hands to onlookers. As you walk down the aisle, admired by all, the fingernails of your two hands should meet in the center of that broad flower stalk, your thumbs steadying the arrangement. Imagine placing your hands together in prayer and curling your fingertips back to meet.

This display takes place at the waistline, the crown of your bouquet will rise above your beautiful hands and leave plenty of clearance for people to admire the neckline of your gown, and your swanlike neck rising to a perfectly coiffed and made-up countenance.

Let your bouquet remind you to breathe. Breathing deeply is the key to relaxing and standing up straight is the key to breathing properly. Use the fragrance of the bouquet as a reminder to practice good posture. This will improve your overall appearance and enable more graceful movement, warding off trips and missteps.

Lilies of the valley top a silver tussie-mussie.

Tossing the Bouquet

The tradition of tossing the bridal bouquet is said to originate in England, where it was hoped that a bride could thus pass on her good fortune. In Medieval Europe, people would to try to rip away pieces of the bride's clothing and flowers—the shreds were believed to be tokens of luck and fertility.

To preserve their dresses, brides started tossing other tokens, like the bouquet in her hand, to lure would-be snatchers away. Today, a staged bouquet toss is a standard part of a wedding celebration: the bride turns her back to give everyone a fair chance and tosses the bouquet over her shoulder to a group of unmarried women who are lined up to try and catch the bouquet. It's said that the woman who catches the bouquet will be the next to marry.

Throwing things at weddings must be a primal urge. A bride in old England would have thrown a shoe at the bridesmaids to select the next to marry. This followed a ceremonial tap with a shoe wherein the groom would symbolically establish his dominance over the new bride. In fact, lots of shoes flew about at Elizabethan weddings. Shoes were thrown after the bride as she left to symbolize transference of the father's authority over the bride to the new husband. Shoes were also thrown at the carriage bearing the bride and groom away, and if they, or their carriage, were hit, it bestowed good luck upon them. This evolved into tying shoes to the back of the carriage, and then tin cans to the back of the wedding car.

Ancient Pagan ceremonies showered grains, nuts, and fruit on newlyweds, "watering" them with food to help new life spring from them in the form of children. In fact, showers of candied almonds are still integral to Greek and Italian weddings. And the word for confetti has its roots in the Italian description of the edible mix used to bless couples. The tradition of throwing rice has its roots in Asia, and symbolizes wishes for prosperity and an abundance of food for the bride and groom.

Contemporary weddings in the West are moving away from rice as eco-conscious guests and irritable grounds managers are encouraging the use of birdseed instead of rice. After the guests have gone, birds happily arrive to clean up the mess. Others offer bubbles for guests to blow, leaving nothing but a wet circle behind.

CARING FOR BODY FLOWERS

Caring for Body Flowers

- TRACY GOODMAN
Side Effects Flowers

Wearing flowers for daytime or evening occasions is fashionable and fun. Body flowers, including corsages and boutonnières can also be worn in the hair, on a collar, on the waist, or on the shoulder. Use them to decorate a purse or even perk up your shoes. But remember, always wear them the way the flowers grow—blossoms up and stems down.

Guard your flowers carefully against sudden exposure to cold air. In very cold weather, carry your body flowers in a box. Put them on after you arrive for the festivities. And remember, too much handling bruises delicate petals and stems. To keep body flowers fresh and bright for a second day, cover them with wet cotton or a thin wet cloth and refrigerate in the florists box. Orchids are the exception to this rule. Unwind the stem wrapping and place the orchid stem in water. Keep in a cool place, out of drafts, but not in the refrigerator.

*People from a planet without flowers
would think we must be mad with joy
the whole time to have such things about us.*

—IRIS MURDOCH
A Fairly Honourable Defeat

A Primer for Handy Maids

WITH BILL MURPHY

*I*t's unlikely that a bride will fashion her own bouquet, arrangements for the bridesmaids, the corsages and boutonnières, and table centerpieces and other floral displays. It's simply too time consuming and she has so many other things to take care of.

Your floral designer is likely to begin preparations at 2 A.M. on your big day—a time when your beauty rest is critical. But for the truly ambitious, you can make a bouquet a day or two in advance, store it in the refrigerator, and pull it out the morning of the event to be wrapped in satin in preparation for your procession down the aisle.

For the determined do-it-yourselfer, we have a few ideas for creating stylish boutonnieres, corsages, and even tussie-mussies for the honored men and women at the ceremony.

What's in a name?
That which we call a rose,
by any other name
would smell as sweet.

- WILLIAM SHAKESPEARE
Romeo and Juliet

Caring for Cut Flowers

A little extra care can make a big difference for any size flower arrangement or fresh flower bouquet. Most floral arrangements last four to seven days, or longer, depending on the flowers used and the care they receive. The Society of American Florists provides these tips for longer-lasting, more vibrant flowers.

One When selecting flowers, look for firm, upright petals and buds just beginning to open. Leaves with spots, yellowing, or a drooping appearance indicate that the flowers have been cut for too long.

Two As soon as you get the flowers home, clean your vessel with an antibacterial solution and prepare your vase with a solution of warm water and flower food. Tracy Goodman of Side Effects Flowers advises using flower food provided by your florist, and says that it does make flowers last longer. But it's important to follow the mixing directions on the flower food packet. Most packets are to be mixed with either a pint or a quart of water. Flower foods should not be diluted with more water than is specified on the packet. If the flower food solution becomes cloudy, replace it entirely with properly mixed flower food solution.

Three Now, cut your stems with a sharp knife or bypass pruner at an angle, and under water if possible. It's important that your implement is sharp so it does not crush the stems. Also note that when your flowers are out of water it takes less than a minute for the stems to close up, loosing their ability to take in water. Re-cutting is necessary for the longevity of your flowers.

Four Finally, remove leaves that will be below the waterline. Leaves in water promote bacterial growth that may limit the flower's ability to take in water. Flowers should be loose in the vase, not packed together. The water should be refreshed or changed every 24 hours. If possible, re-cut stems daily by removing one to two inches with a sharp knife.

Five Keep flowers in a cool spot (65-72 degrees Fahrenheit). Do not store in direct sunlight, near heating or cooling vents, directly under ceiling fans, or on top of televisions or radiators. Appliances like televisions give off heat, which causes flowers to dehydrate. Most flowers will last longer under cool conditions.

Tying a Bouquet

Starting with three dozen roses, strip away the leaves and outer guard petals. If the roses have thorns, remove these as well. Use a knife to cut thorns from stems. Practice this skill with sticks until your hands become adept. The first four roses are set at right angles. Each time you place a rose it goes on an angle.

Place the roses around this center point, rotating and working around the bouquet. This creates a spiral. The bottom should be just as beautiful as the top.

While they are loose in your hand, adjust the roses to create a nice crowned effect.

Use papered wire to wrap the stems at the tightest gathering point. Finish with a knot. You can add foliage at this point.

Using a sprig of Italian ruscus, create a ring around the bouquet by intertwining the stems.

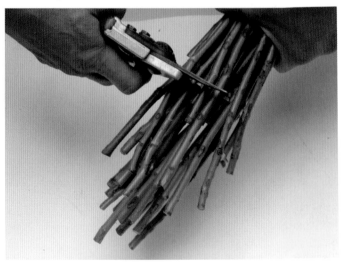

Twist the stems into a solid column and cut the bottoms to a uniform length.

A well-constructed bouquet stands on its own. Store it in a vase to keep the flowers fresh.

Fold the ribbon around toward yourself, wrapping the stems and making sure the wrinkles and folds are smoothed as you go.

Use a two-foot long ribbon to finish the bouquet. First, place the ribbon along the length of the stems.

When you get to the top, tie the ribbon with a double knot pulled tight.

You can leave the ribbon long and trailing, or cut it off at the knot and tuck the knot into the ribbon.

Wire is the contemporary base of choice for corsages and matching boutonnières.

CORSAGE & BOUTONNIÈRE PROJECTS

A bride's bouquet might be stored for several days in the refrigerator prior to the big event. Here are other make-aheads that, with floral preservative spray and refrigeration, can be done a day or two in advance depending on the type of flowers. For determined crafters, much of the work can be done ahead, with the flowers added at the last minute.

DAISY RING

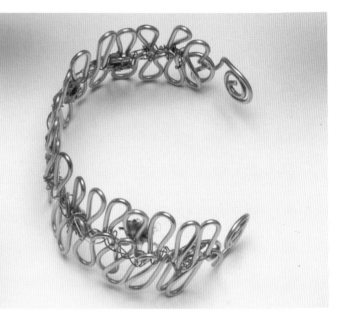

Bracelet like this can be used time and time again for corsages. If you look closely, you can see the dried bases of flowers that previously graced this form. Fresh ones can be glued right over top.

Using 12 gauge aluminum wire, create a "Z"-shaped kink 3 or 4 inches from the end of the wire. Bend a zigzag formation by hand. It should be 5-6 inches long, enough to go almost all the way around the wrist. Cut near the last zigzag and make a matching piece with the same height and length.

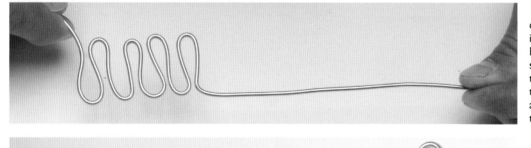

With the two long ends extending out either side, blend the two pieces together, interweaving the loops.

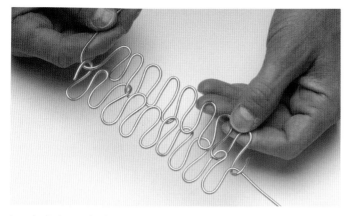

Interlock the ends, closing the short end around the long one to lock it in place.

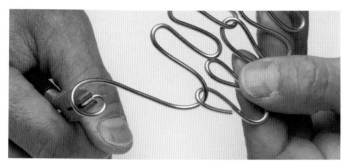

Using flat jewelry pliers, make a swirl with the longer ends on either side.

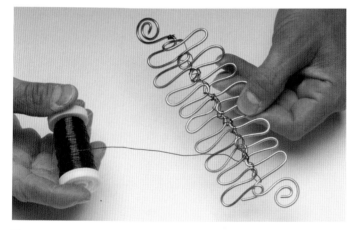

Using a finer, 28 gauge wire, wrap the two pieces and lock them together.

Using the flower of your choice, remove the stems and apply floral adhesive to both the base of the flower and a good connection spot on the bracelet.

Attach Italian ruscus leaves as accents.

A simple "S"-shaped swirl of wire creates a matching boutonniere.

Bridesmaid, groomsman, and in-laws are ready to go. For a flower girl, the bracelet could be quickly fashioned into a cute little hairpiece.

SPARKLING CORSAGE

Here is a more abstract wire frame, reinforced with beaded wire that adds drama to the corsage.

Glue on stock florets along with Italian ruscus leaves.

The finished corsage. The beads bob gently when you move your arm, making a mesmerizing focal point.

"Oh, my love's like a red, red rose, that's newly sprung in June."

—ROBERT BURNS
A Red, Red Rose

TUSSIE-MUSSIE

Place wired crystals, daisies, coxcomb, and Italian ruscus leaves into a standard tussie-mussie holder.

Use floral tape to bind a small bouquet together. Measure the stems before cutting so the arrangement will fit in the tussie-mussie holder, and then wrap the sides and bottom of the stems with tape.

Floral adhesive and pins secure the arrangement to the holder.

A tussie-mussie makes a nice hand-held arrangement for a mother or mother-in-law.

www.littlelightphoto.com

"Perfumes are the feelings of flowers."

-HEINRICH HEINE
The Hartz Journey

Bouquets by Hue

One of the first decisions to make for the big event is the color theme. From bridesmaid dresses to table decor; the colors can reflect the season and the bride's tastes. Naturally, the colors of the bouquet and other flower arrangements have to be a part of that decision. Luckily, roses, lilies, mums, and other flowers have been developed to suit almost any color decision. Season, of course, will dictate availability. Your florist will help you pair favorite colors and flowers with your budget for the event.

Before the color of the traditional wedding gown was whittled down to white in the West, an old English poem laid out other choices for women, though blue seems to be the only other pleasant option:

> Married in white, you will have chosen all right.
> Married in grey, you will go far away.
> Married in black, you will wish yourself back.
> Married in red, you will wish yourself dead.
> Married in blue, you will always be true.
> Married in pearl, you will live in a whirl.
> Married in green, ashamed to be seen.
> Married in yellow, ashamed of the fellow.
> Married in brown, you will live out of town.
> Married in pink, your spirits will sink.

Many brides today spend $1,000 or more on a dress they will wear one day only. More often than not it will be white, so color choices are then left to flowers and the wedding party's attire.

The following are bouquets that represent colorful combinations to contemplate. Organized by color, they present a huge selection of different flowers, including all your favorites, along with what can be expected to be in season on the date of your event. We start out with traditional bridal white and continue through bouquets that are virtual explosions of color.

WHITE IS...

Purity, innocence, and virginity. Strictly speaking, white is not a color, it's the absence of color. Wearing white at one's wedding became popular after Queen Victoria made that choice when she wed Prince Albert in 1840. As the Victorians of the turn of the century sought to emulate this prim and proper queen, it seemed only fitting to follow her nuptial choices as well. Those with a more conspiratorial bent have surmised that the popularization of white helped merchants feed conspicuous consumption among a growing middle class, pushing lace sales and hawking clothing items that would quickly become stained and spoiled, eliminating them from the wardrobe.

A white rose given symbolizes the purity of new love.

www.fleursfrance.com

Artist i Photography

Artist i Photography

Artist i Photography

"The 'Amen!' of nature is always a flower."

–OLIVER WENDELL HOLMES

Artist i Photography

Artist i Photography

Artist i Photography

Artist i Photography

BOUQUETS BY HUE

Pink is...

Pink came to be associated with femininity in the latter half of the 20th Century. Pink is cotton candy, bubble gum, and little girls. Pink ribbons evoke the fight against breast cancer. The first pink Cadillac was created in 1968 as an incentive for great Mary Kay cosmetics saleswomen. Pink complexions epitomize beauty and health.

A pink rose given means,
"I will never forget you."

www.arturovera.com

Artist i Photography

A bouquet proceeds the bride down the aisle, acting as her introduction, and occupying nervous hands while her father steadies her arm.

Donna Theimer AIFD, ICPF

"The flower is the poetry of reproduction.
It's an example of the eternal seductiveness of life."

- Jean Giraudoux

Artist i Photography

Tulip hybrids rise above a pink bed of roses and hydrangea.
Artist i Photography

Artist i Photography

www.fleursfrance.com

www.fleursfrance.com / *Celeste Photo Art*

www.sideeffectsflowers.com

www.sideeffectsflowers.com

www.sideeffectsflowers.com

Pink calla lilies collared in a ring of scarlet peonies. www.sideeffectsflowers.com

BOUQUETS BY HUE

A prelude to a tropical honeymoon, enormous orchids are worthy of a raised glass. *www.kimlemaire.com*

Gerber daisies star in a pink bouquet. www.sideeffectsflowers.com

www.nimagery.com

Pink peonies with green hydrangea accents. www.fleursfrance.com

Artist i Photography

Artist i Photography

Pink cymbidium brings exotic flair to a bridal bouquet.
www.fleursfrance.com

Berries add the appeal of natural gems to a pink rose bouquet.
www.fleursfrance.com

www.fleursfrance.com

www.kimlemaire.com

Red is...

Hot, passionate, and powerful. Red is Cupid and the devil. Scientists have found that red can raise blood pressure and your rate of respiration. Red flags signal warnings and "seeing red" implies anger. In the West, a red suit or tie confer power, while for many years a woman in red clothing (or a scarlet letter) conveyed a symbol of sin.

In the East, red is the color of happiness, prosperity, and celebration, the natural choice for a blushing Chinese bride to wear to her wedding.

And in the West we paint the town red when we want to celebrate, and roll out a red carpet for dignitaries. A bride who chooses red for her flowers is willing to grab attention and stand out. A little red goes a long way, best illustrated by a red bouquet contrasted with the white of a wedding gown. Maybe this is what you want on your red letter day!

Donna Theimer AIFD, ICPF

A red rose given indicates passionate love.

Artist i Photography

Artist i Photography

Artist i Photography

www.sideeffectsflowers.com

www.fleursfrance.com / *Jules Bianchi Photo*

Donna Theimer AIFD, ICPF

Artist i Photography

Artist i Photography

Artist i Photography

PURPLE IS...

Purple is the color of imagination and art, alternative lifestyles, and at one time, great wealth and power. Purple is the color of British Royalty and Elizabethan laws forbade all but those with the highest social standing from wearing the color. Purple is a balanced color, made from the combination of red and blue, the warmest and coolest primary colors. Purple roses symbolize eternal love, paternal or maternal love, protection, enchantment, royalty, and majesty.

The gift of a purple rose symbolizes eternal love.

"Black" calla lilies push the definition of red into its deepest velvet hues. www.fleursfrance.com / *Blondin Photography*

Artist i Photography

Artist i Photography

"I perhaps owe having become a painter to flowers."

—CLAUDE MONET

www.nimagery.com

www.fleursfrance.com

www.fleursfrance.com

www.fleursfrance.com

Artist i Photography

LAVENDER IS...

Suggesting refinement and grace, lavender has long been a favorite color among genteel ladies. It's the grown-up pink, a feminine shade that implies the fragrant blooms of lavender and lilac. It encompasses all the yummy associations you have with plum, orchid, violet, and mauve. It's purple, refined by your comfort level within a great range of lighter shades.

When a lavender-colored rose is given,
it symbolizes love at first sight,
birth of infatuation.

Artist i Photography

www.kimlemaire.com

"*A flower's fragrance declares to all the world
that it's fertile, available, and desirable,
its sex organs oozing with nectar.
Its smell reminds us in vestigial ways of fertility,
vigor, life force, all the optimism, expectancy,
and passionate bloom of youth.
We inhale its ardent aroma and,
no matter what our ages,
we feel young and nubile
in a world aflame with desire.*"

-DIANE ACKERMAN
A Natural History of the Senses

Artist i Photography

BLUE IS...

Something old, something new, something borrowed, something blue is an old English rhyme whose first three items are symbols for continuity, optimism, and borrowed happiness, while the color blue represents purity, love, and fidelity.

The blues of the sky and oceans are calming—their seemingly infinite height and depth have long inspired spiritual and mystical symbolism in many cultures. Scientists have also measured blue's calming qualities. Blues in uniforms and business suits portray power and importance, while royal blue signifies wealth and the ability to obtain indigo and other rare dyes.

Since a truly blue rose is only a fantasy, it thus symbolizes the unattainable.

www.kimlemaire.com

Artist i Photography

*"The world is a rose;
smell it and pass it to your friends."*

—PERSIAN PROVERB

www.sideeffectsflowers.com

A trio of bouquets for bride and maids.   www.fleursfrance.com

www.fleursfrance.com

Artist i Photography

Florists can procure blue roses for you, but they will be artificially colored with blue dye or spray paint.

www.arturovera.com

GREEN IS...

Green is the color of money, growth, and prosperity. In the 15th century, green was the preferred color for a bride's gown—a symbol of fertility and new beginnings. It's also a restful color, with the same calming attributes associated with blue. Though green has long been associated with jealousy and inexperience, it's also the popular symbol of an international movement toward sustainable practices, representing the health of the planet and its occupants.

www.fleursfrance.com

A green rose symbolizes new beginnings and fertility, the perfect accompaniment for a bride stepping eagerly toward life with a new family.

www.littlelightphoto.com

www.littlelightphoto.com

"To analyze the charms of flowers is like dissecting music;
it's one of those things which it's far better to enjoy,
than to attempt to fully understand."

-HENRY T. TUCKERMAN

www.fleursfrance.com

www.fleursfrance.com

www.fleursfrance.com

www.fleursfrance.com

www.sideeffectsflowers.com

www.fleursfrance.com

www.fleursfrance.com

BOUQUETS BY HUE

YELLOW IS...

Yellow roses didn't become popular until the 18th century, after the stigma of jealousy and cowardliness associated with the color began to fade. Today a yellow bouquet symbolizes friendship, and the color evokes cheerfulness. Yellow is the color of sunshine and is associated with joy, happiness, and energy. Yellow is an attention getter. In heraldry, yellow indicates honor and loyalty.

A yellow rose is a symbol of friendship.

Artist i Photography

Artist i Photography

Artist i Photography

"The earth laughs in flowers."

-RALPH WALDO EMERSON

Yellow calla lilies nest in a frame of tropical foliage.

Orange is...

While red is associated with fire, orange is more closely connected with the benign warmth of the sun. Orange is spicy and creative, and slightly mischievous given its close association with Halloween. In flowers, the combination of red (love) and yellow (friendship) are combined within orange blooms to create the perfect partnership.

Coral or orange roses denote enthusiasm and desire.

www.arturovera.com

Artist i Photography

Artist i Photography

"We can complain because rose bushes have thorns, or rejoice because thorn bushes have roses."

—ABRAHAM LINCOLN

www.fleursfrance.com / Nick Brown Photography

www.kimlemaire.com

www.fleursfrance.com / Richard Wood Photo

www.fleursfrance.com

BOUQUETS BY HUE

Artist i Photography

"Where flowers bloom so does hope. "

—LADY BIRD JOHNSON
Public Roads: Where Flowers Bloom

RIOTOUS BLENDS AND EXOTIC MIXES

Riotous Blends and Exotic Mixes

Traipse through a garden of bouquets, where the entire rainbow has been bound up in ribbons. Here is an exciting and vivid gallery of wonderful flowers. Watch for the unexpected, like feathers, grasses, sparkly gems, and even a touch of iridescent paint. Imagine what you could do with your favorite blooms to express your personality and the season.

RIOTOUS BLENDS AND EXOTIC MIXES

Artist i Photography

Artist i Photography

Artist i Photography

Artist i Photography

www.sideeffectsflowers.com

www.sideeffectsflowers.com

www.sideeffectsflowers.com

www.sideeffectsflowers.com

RIOTOUS BLENDS AND EXOTIC MIXES

CASCADES

These wonderful sprays of flowers are a traditional favorite and are making a comeback. They make an unforgettable statement, but have one drawback—they are a bit heavy and hard to set down. Unlike a hand-tied bouquet, you can't just set a cascade down on a table or chair and snatch it up on the fly. Still, nothing can compare to the beauty of a bouquet that cascades from waist to kneecap. Moreover, the shape can add stature and slenderize the bride. In other words, it's worth the pain!

Artist i Photography

www.sideeffectsflowers.com

www.kimlemaire.com

79

Exotics

Donna Theimer, AIFD, ICPF

Feathers and wisps of willow add allure to a red bouquet.
Donna Theimer, AIFD, ICPF

Fern fronds and red foliage add tropical elements to a calla lily bouquet.
www.sideeffectsflowers.com

Wheat and seed-bearing grasses hark back to ancient nuptial bouquets, which expressed a wish for prosperity and plenty. www.sideeffectsflowers.com

Succulents make this calla lily bouquet a bit different.

"*When you take a flower in your hand
and really look at it,
it's your world for the moment.
I want to give that world to someone else.
Most people in the city rush around so,
they have no time to look at a flower.
I want them to see it
whether they want to or not.*"

— Georgia O'Keeffe

Spray paint is one of the hottest trends in floral design. Tweaking nature's art just a little adds eye-catching appeal. *www.bristolfoto.com*

Lotus root, exotic berries, and blooms cap a beaded wand.
Donna Theimer, AIFD, ICPF

Blue elements create fireworks-like appeal for a July 4ᵗʰ bride.
www.fleursfrance.com

A fan ads Asian flair to a bridal bouquet.
Donna Theimer, AIFD, ICPF

Cast iron plant leaves create an exotic nest for calla lilies in this beautifully bound bouquet. www.sideeffectsflowers.com

Peacock features jut from a white rose and calla lily bouquet accented with astilbe. www.fleursfrance.com

Dried lotus root and fern shoots add exotic elements to green hydrangea.
Artist i Photography

Flowering grasses drape the sides of this tightly crowned bouquet of roses and berries. www.sideeffectsflowers.com

www.nimagery.com

"Flowers are love's truest language."

-Park Benjamin

Bridesmaids All in a Row

Early wedding planners had different items on their event checklists. For example, preventing evil spirits from ruining the wedding. Apparently weddings were viewed as prime targets for wicked entities. To ward them off families would hire pretty girls and dress them in finery to confuse the bad spirits. So, bridesmaids were glorified decoys, who had to be rewarded for this high-risk employment.

Today bridesmaids are still dressed in finery, and usually rewarded with some token of appreciation from the bride. They also function as friends and helpers to the bride, contributing to the preparations and providing much needed moral support.

The bridesmaids' bouquets may match the brides, or act as foils to them. This chapter illustrates the many options available to brides outfitting her wedding party with flowers.

"Are we, finally, speaking of nature or culture when we speak of a rose (nature), that has been bred (culture) so that its blossoms (nature) make men imagine (culture) the sex of women (nature)? It may be this sort of confusion that we need more of."

— MICHAEL POLLAN
Second Nature

www.fleursfrance.com / *Jeffrey Davilla Photo*

Artist i Photography

Artist i Photography

Artist i Photography

BRIDESMAIDS ALL IN A ROW

www.fleursfrance.com / *Jack Hecker Photo*

www.fleursfrance.com

www.kimlemaire.com

www.fleursfrance.com

Artist i Photography

Artist i Photography

Artist i Photography

Artist i Photography

www.sideeffectsflowers.com

www.arturovera.com

BRIDESMAIDS ALL IN A ROW

Artist i Photography

Artist i Photography

Artist i Photography

Artist i Photography

Donna Theimer, AIFD, ICPF

BRIDESMAIDS ALL IN A ROW

www.fleursfrance.com / *Celeste Photo*

www.fleursfrance.com / *Blondin Photography*

www.fleursfrance.com / *Blondin Photography*

www.arturovera.com

Artist i Photography

Artist i Photography

Artist i Photography

Artist i Photography

Artist i Photography

The Groomsmen's Lapels

The tradition of the groom's flower display stems from a Medieval tradition wherein a knight wore his lady's colors in declaration of his love. The groom's boutonniere traditionally displays a flower found in the bridal bouquet.

"Let us open our leaves like a flower,
and be passive and receptive."

-JOHN KEATS

Artist i Photography

www.fleursfrance.com

Pink ranunculus adorns the boutonnière on the left, bells of Ireland the arrangement on the right. www.fleursfrance.com

Donna Theimer, AIFD, ICPF

A boutonnière acts as secure conduit for the nuptial rings.

www.arturovera.com

www.fleursfrance.com

Artist i Photography

Artist i Photography

Artist i Photography

www.nimagery.com

www.arturovera.com

www.fleursfrance.com

www.fleursfrance.com

www.nimagery.com

www.fleursfrance.com

www.fleursfrance.com

www.fleursfrance.com

Artist i Photography

THE GROOMSMEN'S LAPELS

www.fleursfrance.com

www.fleursfrance.com

www.fleursfrance.com

www.fleursfrance.com

www.fleursfrance.com

www.fleursfrance.com / *Richard Wood Photo*

THE GROOMSMEN'S LAPELS

Artist i Photography

www.fleursfrance.com

Artist i Photography

www.fleursfrance.com

Artist i Photography

Artist i Photography

Artist i Photography

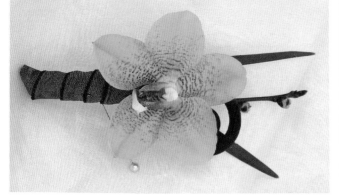

An artichoke provides an exotic centerpiece for this green boutonnière. www.fleursfrance.com

www.fleursfrance.com

www.fleursfrance.com

www.fleursfrance.com

www.fleursfrance.com

www.fleursfrance.com

Artist i Photography

www.fleursfrance.com

www.fleursfrance.com

www.fleursfrance.com / *Michelle Walker*

www.fleursfrance.com

www.fleursfrance.com

www.fleursfrance.com

Artist i Photography

FLOWER GIRLS

Flower Girls

In the Middle Ages, young girls were sent ahead of the bride and groom to cast grain on the ground, ensuring the couple's prosperity and fertility. Flower petals probably grew out of another European tradition wherein the mother would release flower petals over her newly married daughter's head to ward off evil. A lovely young girl, dressed like a princess, parading in front of your guests is too endearing to need any further meaning today. Here are some ideas for adorning your flower girls.

Artist i Photography

"*It will never rain roses. When we want to have more roses, we must plant more roses.*"

−George Eliot

www.fleursfrance.com / *Ken Viale Photo*

Artist i Photography

www.fleursfrance.com

www.fleursfrance.com

www.fleursfrance.com /
Dennis Urbiztondo Photo

Artist i Photography

Artist i Photography

Artist i Photography

www.fleursfrance.com / *Laver Studios Photo*

Artist i Photography

www.sideeffectsflowers.com

www.fleursfrance.com / *Blondin Photography*

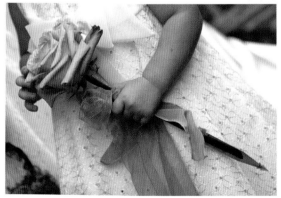

www.fleursfrance.com / *Lisa Leigh Photo*

Artist i Photography

www.fleursfrance.com

www.fleursfrance.com

www.fleursfrance.com / *www.thebecker.com*

www.fleursfrance.com

www.fleursfrance.com

Artist i Photography

Ring Bearers

The ring bearer is a relatively new tradition with roots in a Victorian practice in which a boy and girl were dressed as a wedding couple and paraded down the aisle for everyone's amusement. A miniature bride and groom offered comic relief during the long wait for the event to begin, and lightened the mood prior to the long ceremony to follow. Generally the real rings are kept in the secure possession of the groom's best man, while faux rings are attached to a pillow for the young ring bearer to carry to the altar. If the ring bearer does in fact have the real rings, they are usually tacked down with thread to prevent their loss. The following images display several different styles of ring pillows, another important floral component for your big day.

www.fleursfrance.com

"Flowers bring to a liberall and gentlemanly minde, the remembrance of honestie, comelinesse and all kindes of virtues."

– John Gerard

Artist i Photography

"Flowers leave some of their fragrance in the hand that bestows them."

— CHINESE PROVERB

Corsages for Special Ladies

Ladies wear delicate silk and satin dresses to weddings. If you honor them with flowers, you could be asking them to damage their clothing if they need to pin it on. Thus special wedding guests are given flowers they can wear on their wrists, freeing them from the burden of having to carry a bouquet. Traditionally, mothers of the bride and groom are gifted with flowers at the wedding event. Siblings might also be given a corsage, as well as special aunts or very dear friends who are not part of the wedding party. The following examples offer some options for adorning the special ladies at your wedding.

www.nimagery.com

Artist i Photography

Artist i Photography

Artist i Photography

Artist i Photography

CORSAGES FOR SPECIAL LADIES

www.bristolfoto.com

Frequently Asked Questions

- TRACY GOODMAN
Side Effects Flowers

HOW FAR IN ADVANCE SHOULD I CONTACT THE FLORIST WHEN ORDERING WEDDING FLOWERS?

Flowers are one of the most important aspects of your wedding day. They set the mood and tone for the event and will be remembered for years to come. Many florists can accept only a set number of weddings on a given day, so it's important to contact your florist well in advance to begin planning. A good rule of thumb is to contact your florist at least three months in advance. However, if your wedding is going to be an exceptionally elaborate event, take place during peak wedding season, or fall on a holiday, then six months to a year is not too soon to contact your florist. This will allow the florist to begin looking for any props or specialty items you might need. Wedding flowers can be highly specific and colors often have to be very precise, so florists need advance notice to place flower orders.

WILL A FLORIST WORK WITHIN MY BUDGET?

Yes. Be honest about your budget on the initial consultation so the florist knows what to recommend. By taking your budget into consideration from the very beginning of the planning process, the florist can give you the best advise on how to place the flowers for maximum effect and what types of flowers offer the best value and achieve your desired look.

Is it okay to visit several florists to get estimates?

Sure, but tell the florists that you are gathering estimates rather than making an appointment for a consultation. Be prepared with a detailed list of your floral needs. The florist will be able to give a rough estimate without a lengthy meeting. If you are gathering ideas and then comparisons, it's best to inform the florist of your intentions. Floral designers are trained and highly skilled floral artists. Their ideas have value. You may be asked to pay a consultation fee if you want to discuss a florist's actual ideas for your wedding. In most cases, the fee will be applied to the flowers once the order is placed.

What should I bring to the flower shop when I have my wedding consultation?

The more information you can provide the better your florist will be prepared to offer creative suggestions. Your florist wants to create a spectacular and memorable event for you. Anything you can bring will be beneficial. Pictures that depict what you have in mind are extremely helpful. Bring a photo of your dress and a sample of the fabric or lace if you have it, as well as swatches and photos of the bridesmaids' dresses. Also think about what style of wedding you want. If you are not sure, your florist can offer suggestions based on your wedding plans so far.

What can a florist do to help me stretch my ceremony and reception budget?

Besides suggesting specific types of flowers that will work within your budget, a professional florist can offer helpful suggestions as to what flowers might be used at both the ceremony and reception. A few examples: bridesmaids' bouquets can become table decorations, the bride's bouquet can become the head table arrangement, the pew markers can become festive bows on cars or doors, and altar designs can flank the buffet or cake table. Florists are overflowing with creative ways to make use of your budget and flowers wisely.

Artist i Photography

Floral Designers

Tracy Goodman is owner and lead designer of Side Effects. With more than twenty years of experience creating botanical artistry, her specialty is fabulous, custom wedding designs using only the highest quality flowers.

Side Effects
Tracy Goodman
1934 S. Broadway
Denver, CO 80210
1-303-722-1180
www.sideeffectsflowers.com

Bill Murphy, AIFD, ICPF designs for private events, as well as showroom displays, throughout the United States. His work has been featured in The Knot, Floral Design, Modern Bride, and many regional publications.

Cutting Edge Floral Artistry
47 North Duke
York, PA 17401
1-717-676-9009
www.cuttingedgefloral.com

Donna Theimer, AIFD, ICPF is a professor of horticulture at Joliet Junior College in Joliet, IL. She is responsible for teaching four different floral design classes, as well as an assortment of horticultural topics. Additionally, she assists students with the creation of wedding and event flowers for area brides and businesses. She won Best Bridal Bouquet category for the 2006 *Florists' Review* magazine wedding contest. She has created flowers for hundreds of weddings and events with budgets ranging from $350 to $125,000. She was inducted into the American Institute of Floral Designers (AIFD) in 2004 and is an Illinois Certified Professional Florist (ICPF). She has presented many design programs for a variety of professional and community groups and organizations.

Donna Theimer, AIFD, ICPF
Joliet Junior College
1215 Houbolt Ave.
Joliet, IL 60431
1-815-280-2276

Jessica Switala started Fleurs de France nearly 30 years ago and works from her home studio, nestled on a few tranquil acres in Sonoma county. Through exquisite and stunning custom floral design, personalized service, and consistently flawless high quality, Fleurs de France has earned a spot on some of the most prestigious preferred vendor lists on many wedding venue websites in Sonoma and Napa Valley wine country. Fleurs de France is extremely creative and versatile in a wide range of design styles that can be tailored to your taste and event, whether your event is an intimate or lavish soiree, modern or whimsical, sophisticated, romantic, or elegant. For Fleur de France every event is unique and each detail is important, including bouquets, boutonnieres, and centerpieces. Fleur de France sees that they are all pieces of art.

Fleurs de France (FDF)
Sebastopol, CA
1-707-824-8158
www.fleursfrance.com
js@fleursfrance.com

Photographers

Aaron Bristol lives in South Florida and specializes in weddings. He is well versed in many types of photography and capturing moments and savoring memories is his passion.

Aaron Bristol
1-561-929-3308
www.bristolfoto.com
www.eventpictures.com
bristolfoto@aol.com

Cheryl B. Wiles "I find passion and contentment in capturing real moments in people's lives behind my camera's lens. I love to mingle in a crowd at a corporate event and simply enjoy people having fun. I treasure taking maternity pictures and then photos of the new baby. When I receive holiday cards with family portraits I've taken, I feel the joy I capture and the recorded family memories that are shared with others. It's an honor to be involved in two peoples' lives and that of their families' with my photography—from their engagement to their wedding day celebration to their pregnancy and birth of children to family reunions and christenings! I do live a very blessed life taking photographs of all these life cycles in peoples lives."

Artist i Photography
Cheryl B. Wiles
129 South Skyview Drive
Nederland, CO 90466
1-303-258-1411
cheryl@artistiphotography.com
www.artistiphotography.com

Arturo Vera A professional photographer for 20 years, serves all of California and destination weddings. He has received a number of prestigious awards, such as Photographic Technical Excellence and the Silver Cindy from the Information Film Producers of America. He honed his talent and passion for photography in San Francisco, California, at California's Academy of Art, where he received his Bachelor of Fine Arts degree.

Arturo Vera
1-209-460-0780
info@arturovera.com
www.arturovera.com

Kate has been photographing weddings and portraits in her own unique style for more than 10 years. She loves documenting all of the emotions and details that go into a wedding day. She truly feels honored to share in the special moments of her clients' lives. This Little Light Photography is based in North Carolina, but provides services in Indiana and New Orleans, and is available for travel worldwide.

This Little Light Photography
www.littlelightphoto.com
1-317-702-5236
kate@littlelightphoto.com

Nick Blake has been shooting weddings for more than fifteen years in Chicago and the surrounding suburbs, in addition to destination weddings. He studied film at Chicago's Columbia College and commercial photography at the Harrington College of Design. Blake says, "I am always striving to capture the moments that are often overlooked as common; a gesture, a look, a tear. I go into a wedding knowing that these are the images that will be shared for generations and will define a moment in time that is truly significant. It's important to capture not only the activities that take place, but the emotion that was so prevalent at the celebration."

Nick Blake, Photographer
9 Acorn Drive
Hawthorn Woods, IL 60047
1-847-471-1545
www.nimagery.com
nick@nimagery.com

Kim Lemaire "Ever since I was a little girl, I wanted to create beautiful things like all the other women in my family," writes Kim Lemaire about the inspiration for her 20-year career as a professional photographer. "I had to find my own way of creating something beautiful that people would like and enjoy looking at over and over again. Photographing people and things makes me happy—it brings me joy. I want your photos to be something you look at over and over again and make you smile."

Kim Lemaire
PO Box 221184
Carmel, CA 93922
1-831-642-9538
www.ensemble-productions.com
www.kimlemaire.com